**SPORTS** Machines

# Personal Watercraft

By E. S. Budd

The Child's World®

Published by The Child's World®
PO Box 326
Chanhassen, MN 55317-0326
800-599-READ
www.childsworld.com

Design and Production:
The Creative Spark, San Juan Capistrano, CA

Photo Credits: Images on pages 5 (bottom), 6, 8, 15 (bottom), 17, 23 (top) © 2003 Kawasaki Motors
Corp., USA. All rights reserved. All other images © 2003 David M. Budd Photography.

**Library of Congress Cataloging-in-Publication Data**
Budd, E. S.
 Personal watercraft / by E.S. Budd.
   p. cm. — (Machines at work)
Includes bibliographical references and index.
 ISBN 1-59296-163-0 (Library bound : alk. paper)
1. Personal watercraft—Juvenile literature. 2. Jet skiing—Juvenile literature.
[1. Personal watercraft. 2. Jet skiing.] I. Title.
GV840.J4B83 2004
797.3—dc22
                              2003023664

# Contents

# Let's Ride a PWC!

Let's ride a PWC! Personal **watercraft**, or PWC, are designed to be used on water. People all over the world enjoy riding these sport machines. Some people ride them just for fun. Others compete, racing their watercraft at high speeds. It's an exciting action sport.

The first PWC was built by an inventor who wanted to make a powered water ski. It was a small, quick craft built for one person. By the 1970s, companies began to sell similar machines to the public, like the one shown above.

These early machines did not have seats. Riders stood up as they rode them. These PWC required a good sense of balance and took time to learn to ride. Some of today's PWC are a lot like the earliest ones. They are called stand-up models.

Today there are many types of personal watercraft. Most modern designs are made with seats. These sit-down models are easier to ride. Some are big enough for three or four riders.

In fact, the most popular machines are made for two or more people to ride. It's a great way for families to spend time together.

There are many kinds of PWC races. Several riders of the same ability race against each other. They all ride the same kind of machine.

It is very important that all PWC racers have good racing skills. It takes practice to ride a PWC, especially at high speeds. Racers always wear helmets and life jackets for protection.

Racers usually ride PWC made for one person. These machines are lighter and can move more quickly. They can also make tight turns and move in small circles. Riders race on a course set up on the water. They weave quickly around **buoys,** racing to the finish line.

It's exciting to do stunts and tricks on a PWC. Some riders can even take their craft underwater! A PWC can also pull a **wake** boarder or water skier behind it.

Safety is an important thing to keep in mind when riding a PWC. These machines reach speeds up to 65 miles per hour. A **throttle** speeds up the craft. But a PWC does not have a **brake.** To slow down, riders must let up on the throttle.

Sometimes riders cannot stop quickly enough. This can cause **collisions** with objects or other craft. PWC have no sides to prevent a rider from falling off the machine. For this reason, riders must wear a life jacket at all times. Wearing eye protection, shoes, and gloves is also a good idea.

It's challenging to learn how to ride a PWC. Beginners should always take a class before they ride for the first time.

In fact, many experts think a PWC is like a car. Only people over age 16 should drive them. But you can still have fun as a passenger!

# Climb Aboard!

Would you like to see what it's like to ride a PWC? The same things that make personal watercraft fun also make them dangerous—they're small, fast, and open. Always look for swimmers and other craft in the water around you. Don't forget your life jacket! And remember, safety first. Now, let's go have some fun!

A PWC has a gasoline engine. It powers a jet pump that pulls water from under the craft into an **impeller.** The impeller forces water out a nozzle at the rear of the craft. This jet of water moves the craft forward. Riders use handlebars to steer a PWC. A kill switch turns off the engine. Many PWC have a cord connected to the kill switch. Riders attach the cord to their wrist or life jacket. If the rider falls off, the cord is pulled. The engine then stops running.

1. Handlebars
2. Impeller
3. Engine

4. Throttle
5. Kill switch
6. Kill switch cord

# Glossary

**brake (BRAYK)** A brake is a control that helps a rider stop or slow down a vehicle. A personal watercraft does not have a brake.

**buoys (BOO-eez)** Buoys are anchored objects that float in the water, often to warn or direct people in watercraft. Buoys show the location of a PWC race course.

**collisions (kuh-LIZH-unz)** Collisions are crashes in which two vehicles hit each other. Personal watercraft riders must look for objects and other craft to avoid collisions.

**impeller (im-PELL-ur)** An impeller is a type of propeller on a personal watercraft. The impeller moves a PWC forward.

**throttle (THRAWT-ull)** A throttle is a control on a personal watercraft. It helps riders control how fast they go.

**wake (WAYK)** A wake is the trail left behind a moving watercraft. Wake boarding is a sport in which people surf in a craft's wake.

**watercraft (WAH-tur-kraft)** Watercraft are vehicles made to work on water, such as ships, boats, and PWC. Watercraft are also called craft.